Contents

Introduction

Being involved in a street attack is a traumatic experience whatever the situation - whether you are seriously injured, suffer loss of possessions or escape relatively unharmed.

It Happened to Me - Mugged contains the real stories of six young people who have experienced a mugging. They all have very different stories to tell, from being violently attacked by people known to them (Sharea) to being attacked by strangers for a collecting tin (Luke) and a mobile phone (Emma). The last interview is with Denzel, who has been both a mugger and, in the past, a victim. Here, he speaks about what happened when he and his friends mugged someone else.

The interviews are written as closely as possible from the words of the interviewees and are presented in question and answer format. At the end of each interview there are questions to discuss with friends or to help you think about the topic in depth.

In reading the interviews you may feel vulnerable or worried yourself, particularly if you or someone you know has experienced a mugging. It is important to remember, however, that the risk of being a victim of a mugging is fairly low. Nevertheless, it is sensible to take precautions and you may find the following advice useful.

Staying safe when you're out and about

◆ Carry your bag close to you with the opening facing inwards. Carry your house keys in your pocket.

◆ If someone grabs your bag, let it go. If you hang on, you could get hurt. Remember, your safety is more important than your property.

◆ If you think someone is following you, check by crossing the street – more than once if necessary – to see if he or she follows. If you are still worried, get to the nearest place where there are other people – anywhere with a lot of lights on – and call the police. Avoid using an enclosed phone-box in the street, as the attacker could trap you inside it.

◆ Stick to well-lit roads with pavements. On commons and parklands, keep to main paths and open spaces where you can see and be seen by other people – avoid wooded areas. If you wear a personal stereo, remember you can't hear traffic, or somebody approaching behind you.

◆ Don't take short-cuts through dark alleys, parks or across waste ground. Walk facing the traffic so a car cannot pull up behind you unnoticed.

◆ Don't hitch-hike or take lifts from strangers.

◆ Cover up expensive-looking jewellery and don't flash your mobile phone around.

It Happened to

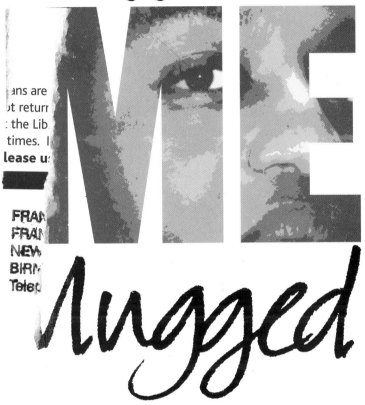

ME

*ans are
ot returr
: the Lib
times. I
lease u:*

**FRAN
FRAN
NEW
BIRN
Telep**

Mugged

Interviews by Angela Neustatter and Helen Elliott

Photography by Laurence Cendrowicz

W
FRANKLIN WATTS
LONDON•SYDNEY

This edition 2005

Franklin Watts
96 Leonard Street
London
EC2A 4XD

Franklin Watts Australia
Level 17/207 Kent Street
Sydney NSW 2000

Copyright © Franklin Watts 2002

ISBN: 0 7496 6236 0
Dewey Classification 364.15'52
A CIP record for this book is available from the British Library

Printed in Malaysia

Interview on pages 34-39 by Helen Elliott, all other interviews by Angela Neustatter

Series editor: Sarah Peutrill
Art director: Jonathan Hair
Design: Steve Prosser
Consultant: Helen Brookes, Royton and Crompton School, Oldham
Photographs: Laurence Cendrowicz, apart from Paul Baldesare/Photofusion: 4b, 14. Nigel Dickinson/Still Pictures: 43. Gina Glover/Photofusion: 10b. Matt Hammill: 34-39. Olly Hoeben: 40, 42, 44. Every attempt has been made to clear copyright. Should there be any inadvertent omission please apply to the publisher for rectification.

With grateful thanks to our interviewees. Also thanks to John Carroll with the Youth Offending Team

If the worst happens

◆ If someone threatens you, shout and scream for help. This may unnerve the attacker and frighten him or her off.

◆ If an attacker asks for your purse or other valuables – hand them over. Your safety is more important.

◆ If you need to, you have a right to defend yourself, with reasonable force, using items that you have with you such as an umbrella, hairspray or keys. The law doesn't allow you to carry anything that could be described as an offensive weapon.

If you have been attacked

◆ A mugging is a serious crime, whether it is committed by a stranger or someone you know.

◆ Call the police straightaway. They need your help to catch the attacker.

◆ Take the name and address of any witnesses.

◆ Try to remember exactly what the attacker looked like.

◆ If a car was involved, try to note the colour, model and registration number.

◆ You do not need to go to the police station to report an assault – you can be interviewed in your own home if you wish. These crimes are dealt with sympathetically, regardless of sex. Police stations have specially trained officers who will help and support you.

◆ Try not to wash at first if you can possibly help it. It will destroy vital medical evidence that will help prove the case against the person who attacked you.

◆ Should your case come to trial, by law you can remain anonymous if you are female, or under 18 years old. The law forbids newspapers to publish anything that might identify you.

◆ It is a good idea to talk to someone about your experience, such as a volunteer from a victim support group.

It Happened to Luke

Luke, 12, was mugged on his eleventh birthday by a group of ten children. He lives with his grandmother and sisters in a quiet suburban area. He was helped by the involvement of a police officer attached to the local Youth Offending Team.

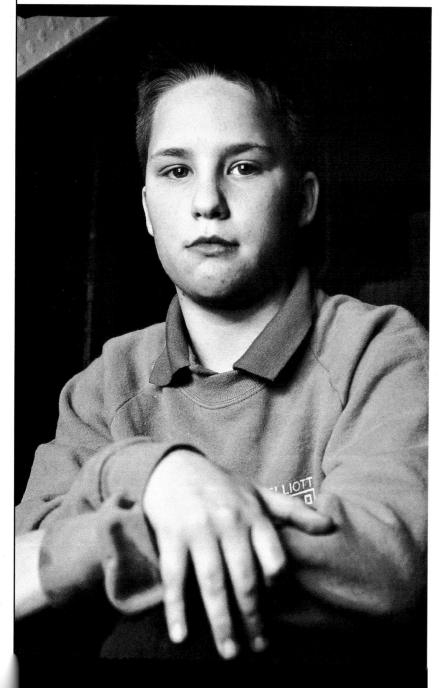

Q What were you doing when you were mugged?

A My birthday is on Hallowe'en. I was out trick or treating with my sisters. I saw a group of kids all quite a lot older than me, probably aged 14 or 15, on the street. I didn't guess they were going to do anything when they came towards me. I didn't know anyone who had been mugged so it wasn't something I thought about.

Q What happened then?

A These kids, boys and girls, started running towards me and my sisters... some of them got hold of my sisters, who are a couple of years older than me, but the others said to leave them alone. One shouted 'there's the boy with the money box' and then they started running towards me. That was frightening... the next thing I knew some of them were spinning me around, trying to loosen my hands on the money box. They flung me on the ground and somebody kicked me quite hard in the stomach. I was in pain and that was when one of the kids ripped the money box out of my hand.

Q How long did this last?

A It happened very quickly - in less than five minutes. I don't remember thinking or feeling anything at the time. I was just aware of it happening and of someone saying 'stop struggling'. Then once they had the money box they ran off fast.

Q Where were your sisters?

A My sisters ran into a friend's house nearby and she ran out and caught one of the group, a girl. She called the police. Then my sisters went to my grandmother's home where we live. My aunts who live close came round too. I told them what had gone on.

Q What happened next?

A The police were called and they came quickly and took me home. My gran was very upset for me - she comforted me and tried to calm me down. She kept asking if I was all right. I felt a bit sick. Afterwards she kept saying it was so wrong that a kid should be set on like that - I'd been so happy with it being my birthday

and Hallowe'en, and I was all dressed up in Dracula clothes. The police advised my aunt to take me to the hospital - I'd been kicked in the stomach and I was bruised - and to have my hand checked. She says I was very shaken and crying - knocked for six - but it's a blur... I don't remember properly.

Q What happened at the hospital?

A In fact there weren't any bad injuries or bones broken in my hand. Although it was bleeding badly I didn't need stitches. They just cleaned it up and bandaged it, but it was very sore.

It's a Fact that...

In the UK violent youth crime has almost doubled in seven years. The number of 10- to 17-year-olds convicted of a serious offence rose from 315 in 1993 to 561 in 2000.

7

Q Were the muggers arrested?

A Only one was caught and she was taken to court. I had to be a witness, which felt weird but I did it and she was found guilty.

Q Did anyone offer you help or counselling?

A A police officer attached to the local YOT (Youth Offending Team) came round to see me. He was very kind and quite gentle and he stayed quite a long

> " John asked whether I wanted to meet with [the mugger] and talk about how it had felt to be a victim but I said no, I just wanted to get over it all."

It's a Fact that...

In 2000 London's Metropolitan Police arrested 20% more street robbers than in 1999.

Cities have higher per capita crime rates than rural areas.

time. He asked what had happened, if he could help at all and he encouraged me to talk. He asked about the group of muggers. I explained that they were at the same secondary school as my sisters and that I was due to go there in September. I think he realised I was bothered that they might attack me again when I went to my new school. It was one of the things causing me anxiety. So John, the police officer, told me he was going to visit the school and make sure that the kids who had attacked me would leave me alone.

Q Did he actually do this?

A John visited the school. He told me later that he met with the girl who was found guilty. He told her how nervous I was about going to my new school - in case the

same kids had it in for me, particularly after the court case. If it happened again he, as the police, would get involved. He told me she seemed quite upset by what she and the others had done. John asked whether I wanted to meet with her and talk about how it had felt to be a victim but I said no, I just wanted to get over it all. I did feel that because he was a police officer he had the power to help me if I needed it in the future.

Q Did you stay off school after the mugging?

A I wanted to get back to school with my friends as quickly as possible. Being with them, telling what happened and them being a bit sympathetic, was a help. I just wanted things to be normal again. They were kind and did my work for

me (I couldn't write with my finger, which was still bandaged from the cuts made when the muggers pulled the tin out of my hand).

Q Were your friends surprised at what had happened?

A My friends were quite shocked because none of them had been mugged, it's not something we expect.

As my gran says, people don't get mugged in this area, so it came as a shock. I think it was just because I was carrying a tin which obviously had money in it. A few months after it happened we went into the local railway station. We saw over the bridge where they had thrown the tin after it had been emptied. That made my stomach turn over a bit.

" My friends were quite shocked because none of them had been mugged, it's not something we expect. "

9

> **" I hoped the kids who had mugged me would just get on with their lives and let me get on with mine. "**

Q When you were starting at secondary school did you feel worried knowing the children who mugged you were pupils there?

A I was nervous but it helped that three of my friends from primary school were also going, and also that my sisters were there. I did feel they would stand up for me if necessary. I hoped the kids who had mugged me would just get on with their lives and let me get on with mine. In fact, none of the kids who mugged me have ever spoken to me even though I sometimes play football with a few of the boys. From what John, the police officer, told me I think they were warned to leave me alone by the headteacher, even though they hadn't been taken to court.

Q Did it take long to get over the mugging?

A It's not easy to forget the violence. I don't like thinking that kids, who in a way are like me, would turn like that. It's not that I expect it to happen all the time, but it's a bit there in my mind. I used to sleep with the light out in my room but I don't like sleeping in the dark now, I ask for the light to be left on

in the hall and my bedroom door open. It just gives me a feeling of being safe. I didn't like going out at night by myself for a while although that is better now. I didn't want to go trick and treating this Hallowe'en so my aunts took me bowling instead.

Q Do your family worry about you?

A My aunts and my gran worry quite a lot when I go out and they are always telling me to be careful. At the same time, my gran says I should be free to walk the streets, it's my right and that only a few bad people behave like the muggers did, most people are honest and good. I tell them not to worry because I think I'm fine now. My gran and my aunt say I'm brave but I don't think of it like that. I'm just getting on with life.

> " I used to sleep with the light out in my room but I don't like sleeping in the dark now ... "

Talking Points

◆ In England, where this attack happened, children aged over 10 are criminally responsible, although under 18s are tried in a youth court. The children who attacked Luke were 14-15. Do you think they were old enough to understand what they were doing? Should young people be treated in the same way as adults or not?

◆ Luke was kicked quite hard in the stomach, but luckily didn't sustain any lasting injuries. Some TV programmes portray this kind of violence routinely and it can look fairly harmless. For example, someone is kicked in the stomach but gets up as if nothing has happened. Do you think this might make some people believe that this kind of attack is not serious? Should TV programmes portray violence more realistically?

It Happened to Emma

Emma is at university in Sussex. She was aged 17, living with her stepmother and going to sixth form in London, when she was mugged a year and a half ago.

Q What time of day did the mugging take place?

A It was ten o'clock in the morning and I was walking up the road to school from Camden Road station. A group of five boys about my age were ahead of me. As I got close they turned and started asking for my name, wanting to know where I went to school, and my telephone number.

Q Did you feel comfortable talking to them?

A I wasn't worried. I answered their questions but then as they went on asking more and being persistent and getting quite familiar obviously wanting to know me, I began to feel a bit nervous. I thought from looking at their clothes and listening to them that they probably came from quite a poor, rough area - I got the impression they weren't in school.

Q What did you do?

A I got out my mobile phone because I thought if I phoned someone and had a chat it would put them off and it would make me

feel better. I realised I was shaking and feeling more nervous... I wanted the boys to go away, but I didn't really think they would do anything to me. I just thought they were chatting me up.

Q What happened then?

A I'd been walking for about five minutes, suddenly, one of the boys grabbed my hand with the phone in it. It was a shock and I loosened my grip without realising so he got it quite easily. I went at him and tried to get the phone back but one of the other guys pushed me off and held my arms. I went on struggling and trying to get my phone, but their manner had changed, they were much nastier and more aggressive now. They were shouting at me to leave them alone and calling me a bitch, that sort of thing. I started crying, saying 'give it back' but they didn't.

It's a Fact that...

In 2001 around 36% of all street robberies in London involved mobile phones. 14- to 17-year-olds are the age group most likely to be victims.

In 2001 London, Manchester, Birmingham, Bristol and Liverpool accounted for 75% of street robberies in England and Wales.

13

A There was nobody walking on the street but there were cars on the road and a man sitting in a van nearby. He seemed to be watching and I hoped he would come and help me, but he didn't do anything... afterwards when I thought about that it was really scary because you think anyone could do anything to you and nobody is going to help you.

Q So the boys had the phone by now and you couldn't get it back?

A The boy who had it ran off and I ran after him up the road leaving the others behind. But by the time I got to my school I hadn't reached him and I realised even if I did I couldn't fight him for the phone. So I ran into school.

Q Were they helpful at your school?

A I was crying, I told them what had happened and they were very kind. They let me sit in the office and they made me herbal tea and phoned my stepmum.

They also immediately phoned the police but they took two hours to come. If they had come immediately they could have caught the boys on the street. Of course they had gone by the time the police arrived. Obviously it wasn't that important to the police, but that just made me feel that there is no protection against mugging. It's so easy for the gangs that do it because they know they can get away with it.

> " ... it was really scary because you think anyone could do anything to you and nobody is going to help you. "

> **"... it seems so bad that street robbers... should learn that people are too frightened to oppose them and that this is a way they can 'earn a living.'"**

Q What did the police do when they came?

A When the police did come they asked for a description. Everything happened quickly, in the space of about a quarter of an hour, and I was not really looking at them. I couldn't give a detailed description - although I might have recognised them if the police had picked them up quickly. Later the police rang me and said to make contact, but I tried several times and couldn't get through. Then I decided there was not much they could do anyway.

Q Did the police give you any guidance on how to avoid being mugged?

A They advised me not to flash a phone around or anything else that might attract muggers and they said it's not wise to fight back when you are mugged. I can see now that it was a dangerous thing to do. People tell you just to hand over whatever you have got because muggers can turn nasty if you don't. But it seems so bad that street robbers, or anyone else, should learn that people are too frightened to oppose them and that this is a way they can 'earn a living'.

Q When did you tell your family about the mugging?

A My stepmother left work and came over to the school immediately to see if I was all right because she was afraid I would be very upset. I said I wanted to stay in school and would be okay. Later that day my mother came

Keeping your phone safe:

◆ Property mark your phone with an invisible marker.

◆ Record the phone's IMEI number - which is unique. If your phone is taken, the number can be used later by police to prove it is stolen.

◆ Be cautious when using your phone in the street, be aware of who is around, especially on busy streets.

◆ Don't flash your phone around unnecessarily.

down from Bath and we met after school. She asked me a lot of questions. We talked about finding a different way of going to school so that I was on a busier road. She said it was better if I didn't chat to boys in groups like that. I also saw that it wasn't sensible to give details of where I'm at school and my name, but at the time it seemed okay.

I thought they might get upset and see me as stuck up and putting them down if I didn't.

Q Were you worried about going to school after what happened?

A I was scared the next day and I would have liked someone to keep me company going to school.

I decided not to walk the same way. I went by tube to a different station so that I walked on a busy street with lots of people around because that felt safer.

Q Has the mugging had a long-term effect on you?

A My brother was mugged in a park when I was

> ## " Now I know it can happen and that makes me feel much less safe on the streets. "

younger. I remember feeling very scared for him afterwards. It brought all that back... it made me feel very vulnerable. Now I know it can happen and that makes me feel much less safe on the streets. Every time I see a group of boys similar to the ones who mugged me my stomach contracts and I get shaky and feel sick. When that happens I try not to get anywhere near them and to change streets if I can. It happened yesterday: I saw two boys on the street looking at me and so I turned round and went back. I don't want boys trying to talk to me again.

Q Did you receive any help or counselling?

A I wasn't offered any help to get over it. I suppose I could have asked but I didn't think of it. I would have liked someone to talk to who is a bit more experienced than my friends.

Q Do you know other people who have been mugged?

A I don't know many girls it has happened to but most of the boys I know have been mugged. What they mostly do, if they are out with girls and have more than £20, is ask the girls to carry their money because it is safer.

Q Have you got over the mugging?

A Moving to university in Sussex and living in Brighton has really made things better. I feel much safer here. There don't seem to be groups of boys like there are in London. I'm enjoying being out on the streets and feeling free to walk around without worrying who is there, in the way I did before I was mugged. And I think time helps you get over it, too.

Talking Points

◆ Emma was not hurt physically in the attack, although she was obviously still very distressed by it. Should such an attack carry the same kind of punishment as a physical one?

◆ Should mobile phone manufacturers try to make phones less attractive to street robbers - by perhaps changing their look or security?

◆ What was the police advice to Emma? Do you think this was useful? What other precautions would be useful?

◆ Emma did not get any counselling after the attack. Do you think it would have helped?

It Happened to Sharea

Sharea, 18, lives with her mother and is training to be a PE instructor. Early one evening she was mugged at her youth club by two girls she knew slightly. This took place nearly a year before this interview but she is still disturbed by what happened.

Q Where were you when you were mugged?

A I was with a friend at the local youth club and we decided to leave at about 7.30 p.m. As we went upstairs, which is the way out, I saw a group of girls, among them two who are a couple of years younger than me but they are bigger than I am. I knew them from on the streets, although I didn't want anything to do with them.

Q Did you speak?

A One of them said she wanted to talk to me. She had been bothering me for the last three months saying she didn't like the way I acted. She and her friends disliked the fact that I go to college and study hard and they are out of school. They say I've got big ideas about myself. I think they are particularly against me because I was far from a perfect child in the past. I used to get into fights and not work much and that kind of thing. But then when I got good grades in my GCSEs I thought I should try to do well and please my mum. Then these girls and people like them started taking the mickey.

But the one who particularly took against me hadn't been on at me for a while, so I thought perhaps she wanted a chat - to say that we should leave the whole thing alone, which was what I wanted.

Q But that wasn't what happened?

A She asked me and my friend to go into a little room that led off the stairway and stupidly we did. When we were in there she said to me, 'Give me what you've got'. She was looking at my new watch and sunglasses which I had bought with money I earned doing a weekend job. Of course I said I wouldn't and I just said, 'I'm leaving'. It was then that she slapped me and the other girl with her came over and they pushed me on to the floor. Then one was kicking me - the other hitting. They stamped on my thighs, kicked me and punched me.

Q What was your friend doing during the mugging?

A She was too scared to intervene. I was frightened too because these things can go too far, these girls have been known to carry knives. My friend was begging the

girls to stop but of course they took no notice. I think she should have tried to do something - I hope I'd have helped her in the same situation. She's less of a friend now than she was.

" My friend was begging the girls to stop but of course they took no notice. "

19

The room where Sharea was mugged holds painful memories for her.

It's a Fact that...

The crimes women commit are more likely to be shoplifting or buying and selling stolen goods than violent offences such as mugging.

Women most likely to commit a criminal offence are aged between 14 and 21.

Q Were you thinking anything while this happened?

A I was very frightened because you don't expect girls to turn on you. I thought I must find a way to escape. I was crouched over trying to protect my face with my hands, but I looked to see where the girls were and then one punched me in the eye and said, 'Stay down'.

Q Did you manage to get away eventually?

A It was in my mind that I must be able to do something. I thought if I counted to three and pushed off I'd have a chance and that's what I did. I think my sudden movement, and I am quite strong, took them by surprise. My friend and I managed to run out of the little room and run home.

Q How long did the whole thing last?

A It was about an hour from when my friend and I left the youth club to arriving home. I got back at 8.30 p.m.

> " I was very frightened because you don't expect girls to turn on you. "

Q What happened when you got home?

A When I got home my mum went ballistic - my dad has never been around and she's on her own. She and my aunt went out looking for the girls but they were gone. She called the police and I went to the police station to make a statement. Later my boyfriend came around. When we went out to get a drink we saw the girls. I ran home and my mum came and flagged down a police car and the girls were arrested.

Q Did you need to go to a doctor?

A I didn't know what they had done to me, but it hurt badly so I wanted to have a doctor check me up. He was really shocked at what they had done. He took photographs of the injuries. I had a bloodshot eye and a bruised face - that was frightening because they could have really damaged my face if they had punched me more before I escaped. I had huge bruises all over my arms and legs and afterwards one leg was badly swollen.

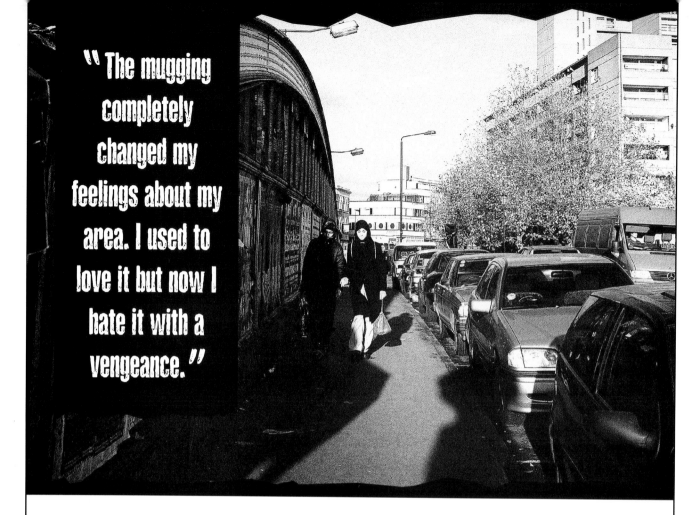

"The mugging completely changed my feelings about my area. I used to love it but now I hate it with a vengeance."

Q Did they take much from you?

A They got a little change and my credit card - they managed to spend £40 on that before I got it cancelled - and they took my new sunglasses.

Q Did you feel nervous being out on the streets after it happened?

A The mugging completely changed my feelings about my area. I used to love it but now I hate it with a vengeance.

All I see is the people hanging out, drugs, robbery and bad behaviour. Immediately after the mugging I left the area and went to live in my sister's flat in Holland Park where I felt completely safe. But then she needed it back and anyway Mum was missing me... it didn't seem fair to leave her on her own.

Q Did your mother worry about you being in the area?

A She applied for a house transfer after the mugging

happened but it didn't happen. I don't really want Mum packing up because of me. She's lived in the same house for 20 years and done it all up herself.

Q The girls were arrested after you saw them, did you want them charged?

A I definitely wanted them charged - I was quite willing to go to court, although quite a lot of people said don't. They were frightened I'd put myself more at risk but I don't believe in being

It's a Fact that...

The British Crime Survey (England and Wales only) revealed that although young men have the highest rate of violent victimisation (8 out of 10 street assaults are against men), mugging victims are divided equally between men and women.

intimidated like that. I felt really angry about what they had done. My mum came with me and the girl who had been the most violent was sitting near me. She kept giving me funny looks. They had social workers not parents with them. They were found guilty and given 100 hours community service and tagged for three months. That means they had to be home by nine o'clock in the evening.

Q Did that make you feel safer?

A Not altogether because I was attacked before nine o'clock so the curfew wouldn't have prevented them mugging me. After the muggers were found guilty I began to get threats from their friends - saying I

would be put in hospital next time they got me. The threats would come through my friends who met the muggers' friends on the street. It does frighten me because these girls don't think, they're very impulsive and just do what they like. The police also see them as dangerous - they've told me. I don't want to have to live like this. It isn't normal.

Q So how do you avoid the girls?

A I am at college across London so I leave early in morning. I'm sure they are not going to be out on the streets at that time. Then I

> **" I just wish it had never happened, that I could wind time back to when I felt safe and happy living my life in my area. "**

work after college, in a shop, to earn money for the things I want and to pay off my credit card. That means I don't get home until after nine o'clock so they have to be home. From what I hear they are keeping to the curfew.

Q How much support have you had?

A My mum's been brilliant and I've had a lot of support from my friends, which obviously helps.

It's a Fact that...

Each year Victim Support offers help to around one million people in England, Wales and Northern Ireland and 40,000 people in Scotland who have been affected by crime. Staff and volunteers are trained to provide emotional support, information and practical help.

And someone from Victim Support came to talk to me. At the time, though, I was in Holland Park in my sister's flat, I was feeling fine and didn't really feel in need of more help.

Q So how has your life changed?

A I don't go out now unless it's with my mum or my boyfriend. That means when I have half term from college I just stay indoors all the time on my own until Mum gets in from work. It's very depressing and boring but I just don't feel safe going out. When the doorbell rings, or I hear noises after it's dark I start to think I'm hearing people breaking in. Or I think I hear my name being called. A couple of times the door bell has rung, but when I go to see who is there there's nobody... that upsets me.

Q What would make things better for you?

A I would like to move out of the area, but I know my mum would be really unhappy if I did. Anyway I can't afford a flat just now. On the other hand, if I could move I could lead a normal life. I don't feel worried on the streets anywhere else, even late at night. I just wish it had never happened, that I could wind time back to when I felt safe and happy living my life in my area.

Talking Points

◆ Sharea was mugged by girls she knew. How did this make her more vulnerable? What do you think their motives were? Do you think attacking someone you know is worse than an ordinary mugging, or not?

◆ Sharea's attackers were caught and sentenced. What was their punishment? Was this a fair sentence in your opinion? Do you think it will help Sharea and her attackers?

◆ Sharea is disappointed about how her friend reacted. Should her friend have helped more? What would you have done?

It Happened to Max

Max, 14, was in his local inner-city park one summer Sunday afternoon, with two friends, when they were approached by a group of boys who mugged them. He identified one of the gang and he will probably be asked to go to court as a witness. This interview took place four months after the mugging.

Q What were you doing before you were mugged?

A I was in the park with my friends just sitting there, hanging out, as we did quite often. I saw two kids, one about 11 the other older, around 17 I would say. They were on bikes and quite close, but I wasn't much bothered by them even though I do know that mugging goes on in the park.

Q So how did this lead to the mugging?

A They came up to us and said, 'Do you have any money?' We just said no. I still didn't feel worried because their manner was quite laid back. Then they said, 'There are two more kids coming and they don't look very happy'. These other two kids came up - one very tall and one other who was a girl of about 16, but she looked like a boy. They started pushing us around and saying they would stab us if we didn't have anything for them. They told us all to roll up our sleeves to see if we had watches. One of my friends did and they told him to take it off which he did.

Q Were they satisfied once they had the watch?

A They wanted more stuff and they were angry with me because I didn't have anything for them. They told me I would have to mug another person and get them something. That really upset me because I don't mug people. I told them I don't do that but they just said again that they would stab me if I didn't. Although they weren't showing knives they were the sort of kids I thought would do it. I've had people mug me in the past a couple of times, but they've always just taken whatever I had or told me to go if I had nothing. This was different... they kept talking about how they would stab us if we didn't get them something.

Q Did they want you to mug someone in the park?

A At first they said I must take a mobile phone lying on the grass behind the woman who owned it. I said I couldn't do that. So then they told me and my friends to go with them down the road. As we walked out of the park I was mouthing 'help' to people, but no-one took any notice. We couldn't get away because the boys were surrounding us. Two were on bikes so they could easily have caught us if we had run. I'm sure they would have beaten us up then.

> " As we walked out of the park I was mouthing 'help' to people, but no-one took any notice."

27

Q Did you feel frightened by this time?

A I felt scared - the scariest thing was not knowing what they were going to do. They told us to try to steal a purse from an old woman but we didn't manage it. Then they started hitting my friend, punching him in the face. One punched me on the nose and I fell to the floor. I felt very upset but they said, 'Don't cry or we'll hurt you'. Then another one kicked me in the head and later when I stood up one of the boys smacked my head against the wall.

Q Even though the idea of mugging someone really upset you, did you feel by this time that you had to do it?

A There didn't seem to be a way of escaping from these boys unless I did what they wanted. There was a woman walking ahead of me and the boys said, 'You have to take that woman's purse, or we really will stab you this time'. So my friend walked close to the woman, grabbed her purse and ran off. She phoned the police on her mobile and ran after him shouting. Then a man coming up the road caught my friend and held on to him. The boys realised they couldn't get the purse then so they tried to make out they had nothing to do with it. They gave the woman back her purse and punched my friend, pretending it was because he had stolen the purse.

Q Did you see anyone who could help?

A I ran up to a car which had stopped and there was a man in it. I asked him, 'Please can you take me to the police station. My friend is going to be hurt and we

will be stabbed.' But he didn't want to know, he just said he wouldn't. My mum was very angry about that afterwards. She kept saying it's a terrible world when adults won't help kids in trouble. The police cars arrived and we ran away from the boys up the hill. The police cars stopped near us and we got in.

Q Because your friend had taken the woman's purse, even though he didn't want to, were you worried the police would treat you as criminals?

A We explained to the police what had happened and they could see we were upset, particularly my friend who had taken the purse. I think they believed us. They took us to the police station to make witness statements saying what had happened to us.

Q Did your parents come to the police station?

A The police phoned them and my mum came to be with me until the police had finished interviewing. I told her all that had happened. She said I must tell the police exactly what I had told her. There was a very nice Asian policewoman who was

29

It's a Fact that...

London police saw an increase in 2001 of young criminals, many as young as 10, committing street robberies because they believe it will give them credibility and status in neighbourhoods they regard as 'lawless'.

very kind and sympathetic. And the police said we had done the right thing going along with what the muggers wanted. They said it's possible they did have knives and it's not worth risking making them angry.

Q How were you feeling by this time?

A I remember being a bit shocked but Mum says I was very shocked... I just wanted to sleep. I lay with my head on her knee and she stroked my head and back. Then when the police had finished, it was about 11 o'clock at night. I felt scared coming out of the police station. I was really cold and shivering in the car and Mum wrapped me in a duvet. When we got home I had hot chocolate and then I went to bed.

Q Did you feel worried about going to school the next day?

A I slept late but when I got up I really wanted to go. I just wanted things to be normal, although I did feel a bit nervous going out of the house.

Q How do you feel now?

A I still feel nervous when I'm out. I find myself looking to see if the kind of kids who I think might mug me are around. My friend is more upset and he's still really frightened to go out. I've been back to the park at lunchtimes because it's near my school. There are lots of us there then, but I haven't been at a weekend. I'm particularly nervous of people in designer clothes - I think they must be getting quite a lot of money to afford them. Today I was in the park and there were boys wearing Scott jackets and Reeboks and Adidas things and I just went back to school. I heard later that they had been mugging kids.

It's a Fact that...

Often court appearances can be avoided if the police give a formal caution. This is more common for young people, but it means the offender has to admit guilt and his or her legal guardian has to promise to act as the police wish.

A Almost all my friends have been mugged, and some of us several times. It shocks you and it is frightening, but it's something my friends and I just assume will happen... we have to try to deal with it. Like the police my mum and dad say it's not worth arguing in case they are carrying

" I don't like feeling edgy every time I go out."

knives and decide to use them. They tell me to carry a small amount of money in my purse to give if I am mugged. They told me to open my purse and show that's all I've got and to keep extra money really hidden. I know it makes my mum really angry that mugging has become something kids have to expect. She says it's all wrong that young people are actually attacking their own peers. I wish it wasn't like that. I don't like feeling edgy every time I go out.

Q After you were mugged did anything happen to the boys who did it?

A The police picked some of them up and I had to go to an identification parade at the police station. Some of the boys who mugged us were there behind glass. I was really nervous going to

do that. I felt it was dangerous in case the boy saw us and tried to find us afterwards. Then when we were driving home with my dad in his van we passed one of the kids who had been in the identification parade. He looked straight at us. He definitely saw us.

Q Are the boys being charged?

A I don't know for sure yet, but it seems likely. That means the police would want me to go to court and be a witness... I don't know if I want to do that. Of course I'd like them to be brought to justice, but I am

frightened if I am a witness and they are still free afterwards they might try to find me. I think they are the kind of kids who would take things one step further.

Q Can anyone do anything to make you feel safer?

A The police can't protect me and there's nothing my parents can do. I do worry it might happen again but now I go out with several friends so that there's quite a lot of us. Really it's down to me to take care, but I'm not going to let those muggers stop me leading the life I want.

Talking Points

◆ No-one went to help the boys, although several people were around. Should they have tried to help? What would have been the best way to do this? Why do you think they didn't help? What would you have done?

◆ Max may have to act as a witness. How does he feel about this? Why? What could be done to make it easier for him?

◆ If the muggers are convicted, what sort of punishment do you think they should get? (Look at the fact box on page 42.) What should the sentence depend on?

It Happened to Mardi

Mardi is a freelance graphic designer and artist. She lives in inner-city Melbourne with her partner and her two dogs. Two years ago Mardi was attacked by a man while walking from her house to her boyfriend's house with one of her dogs. It was a path she had walked hundreds of times before and she felt perfectly safe and confident. She is quietly spoken and still finds herself angry when she speaks of her experience of being mugged which, she says, sometimes makes it difficult to find the right words.

Q What time of day did this happen?

A In the height of summer at 9.30 in the evening. I'd arrived home from aerobics and decided to go over to my boyfriend's house to help him do some stuff around his house.

Q You were alone?

A I was with my dog. My street is in a middle-class residential area and there were a lot of people around, walking their dogs or watering their front gardens. I felt very safe. It was a warm summer night. It's a very friendly time of the year and I didn't expect anything like this to happen. I had been living in my house for over eight months so I had walked this path hundreds of times before. It was very familiar.

Q Was the area well lit?

A Well it was pretty dark, but because we were outside houses there was enough light. Normal street lighting.

Q What did you have with you?

A I was carrying a 35-litre backpack with all my possessions in it, clean clothes, books, personal papers, some jewellery, some money and dog bones! I was also carrying a new pair of shoes in a box in a shopping bag. I think I looked like a target.

Q What happened?

A A white sedan drove past and then pulled up in front of me. This really clean-cut young man between the age of 20 and 25 got out and approached me. He didn't look unusual, or frightening, in any way at all.

> " This really clean-cut young man between the age of 20 and 25 ... approached me. He didn't look unusual, or frightening ... "

It's a Fact that...

In Australia in 1998, males aged between 15 and 19 had the highest victimisation rate of any age group for offences against the person. In general, males are more commonly victims of crime than females.

Q Did you feel at all uneasy being approached by a stranger?

A When you're approached by a stranger at night you do feel a little uneasy... but because I was so close to home and had done it so many times before, I wasn't on guard. My dog, Polly, was running ahead of me and didn't suspect anything either. Looking back at it now I feel it was strange because the man was acting strange - he had his hands behind his back.

Q What did the man say?

A He asked me where this particular pub was. He said he had to be there at a particular time, that he was in a hurry. I wasn't sure and I was trying to think where

it was because I'd heard of it. Someone was waiting in the car for him.

I said I didn't know where the pub was but he lingered, hung around. I just started to move away but he said, 'Will you do me another favour?' and he pulled out a knife - I think it was a kitchen knife. He put it to my throat and swore at me, 'Will you take your backpack off or I'll kill you'.

Q What did you do?

A I just did exactly as he said. That's what the police always say to do. He took it and started walking to the car. Then he turned around and pointed to a necklace I was wearing and asked if it was gold. I told him it was pewter. I was really, really furious but I was so scared I just couldn't do anything.

Then a woman's voice called out, 'What are you doing? Hurry up.' She was in the car. He kept walking towards the car and kept turning around looking at me. He got into the passenger seat and it drove off very fast.

And then my dog realised something was up and she started chasing him after he got into the car.

Q Can you remember how you felt when he had the knife at your throat?

A I felt he might kill me. I could feel the blade against my neck. That's why I acted sensibly. I acted fast and did what he wanted. I'm quite surprised I didn't say, 'No,' because I'm quite strong at times... I've had people approach me before for money and I've been strong.

Q What did you do then?

A I just grabbed my dog and ran home and I noticed that suddenly no-one seemed to be about any more. No one in their gardens or with dogs. It was really eerie. I didn't know what to do, I was panicking. I kept thinking, I need help, I need help.

It's a Fact that...

In Australia, 88% of persons aged 18 years and over feel 'safe' or 'very safe' when walking or jogging locally during the day. When walking or jogging after dark, however, only 38% of persons feel 'safe' or 'very safe'.

Q Who was home?

A My flatmate, Lorraine. She opened the door and said, 'Where's your stuff?' and I started crying and was quite hysterical. She had to call the police. I was in a bad way and she had to dry me off with a towel. Lorraine called the police. She spoke to them, she calmed me down. And even before she had finished the phone conversation with the police station two constables had arrived. They took it very seriously.

Q Were the police helpful?

A They were marvellous. They kept calling and they drove me around to a pawn shop to see if I could find any of my stuff - I had quite a lot stolen, my new watch was in my bag. I also had to go and look at identity photos at three different police stations. They think it was probably to do with drugs and that he needed quick cash. They assured me that I'd done the right thing which was to give him my possessions because they could be replaced. My life couldn't.

Q How did you feel the next day?

A The next morning I was supposed to go to look at identity photos but I couldn't leave the house. I was really scared. There was a white car parked outside and I felt extremely paranoid that they had followed me and knew where I lived.

> " [The police] assured me that I'd done the right thing which was to give him my possessions because they could be replaced. My life couldn't. "

37

Q How long did this fear last?

A For a long time. I couldn't even walk on the street by myself for about eight months. Even in the day I couldn't go out alone and I couldn't go out at night at all.

Q So the impact on your life was profound?

A I was doing market research at the time and I couldn't do the night shift. It interfered with my entire life because I had to work around not being alone on public transport and always being picked up.

Now I'm just really, really cautious. I'm practical when it comes to being out. I never make eye contact with people, especially males I see on the street either in the day or night. I cross the street when there's someone coming towards me. I won't give directions to anyone, no matter what they look like. But now, almost two years later, I am starting to walk alone at night - just small distances from the tram to my house. I get paranoid at times.

Q What do you mean by paranoid?

A I get very, very anxious and imagine different scenarios. That somebody's going to pull out a knife and rob me on the tram, for instance. I don't feel secure in many situations.

Q How do you feel towards your attacker now?

A Still incredibly angry. I really look down on young men who I see in groups who remind me of him. I always feel that they're up to no good. I was never like that before this happened. I'm very angry towards people who have drug problems. I don't like feeling this way.

Q What would you say to anyone reading this about their personal safety?

A I'd suggest that young women not be too casual

and not to be too relaxed when anyone approaches, especially at night. But really, in this situation I don't think there's anything you can do. If that happens to you it's going to happen. I'd strongly urge anyone just to do what they want.

Q Has it taken away your general confidence?

A Yes. I'm a lot more timid. My whole freedom has gone. Perhaps it's because I'm a woman. I don't have that physical confidence that I thought I'd have in any situation. When something like this happens you are really put in your place. This might sound as if I'm making women sound inferior, but we are, physically. We don't want to admit it but women are at a disadvantage here.

Q What has helped you get back into normal life the most?

A I've helped myself. I'm good at talking about it. My friends are really good and will listen. My parents were also very good, they sent me money for new shoes and a new backpack and said I'll just have to start again.

I didn't lose much compared to what could have happened and I'm grateful for that. What I lost was trust.

Q If you saw your attacker today what would you do?

A The police advised me to follow him, see where he went and write down the details and call them. But sometimes I think I see him and they're always different people. I'm always searching for him. But you know, if I saw him today I don't know whether I'd even bother calling the police because it was a long time ago. But I am still outraged that he did this to me and it has had such an impact on my life.

Before this happened I marched in a 'Reclaim the Streets' march, because I always understood that women do not have the freedom to walk the streets at night. But it's weird, I never ever thought this would happen to me, never, especially two minutes from my house and especially when you think you live in a safe area.

Talking Points

◆ Mardi felt very safe before the attack. Find at least three reasons for this.

◆ Probably the worst thing about Mardi's experience is not the loss of her possessions but that it has knocked her confidence and left her not trusting people. She is more wary, though, and perhaps less likely to be attacked again. Do you think this is a better way to be than feeling safe as she did before?

39

It Happened to Denzel

Denzel* was 15 when he joined up with a group of friends and mugged another boy. He grew up living with his mother on an inner-city estate. He is now 18 and is serving a sentence for street robbery at a youth prison.
* not his real name.

Q How did you meet the friends with whom you carried out the mugging?

A From the age of ten we lived on an estate and these boys were friends I grew up with. We went out together as a group. Most of us were excluded from school, so we usually went out and stayed up late in the evenings because we didn't have to get up in the morning.

Q How did the mugging happen?

A On this occasion we went to a club where we hung out and talked and drank. It was about midnight when we left and we were fairly drunk. We were outside standing by a taxi rank when a boy we didn't know came up. He was quite confrontational and aggressive in his manner. We were feeling good and we didn't appreciate him coming and deflating our mood. He was bolshie, man, and he pushed into one of our group and he didn't say 'sorry' or anything and that really annoyed us. We said, 'What are you doing? Say sorry,' that kind of thing but he wouldn't. He just said, 'I'm not scared of you'. Then because he wanted to get past and we weren't letting him until he apologised, he hit one of my mates.

Q You could have just gone away and ignored him, couldn't you?

A I suppose we could have just punched him back and let him go but his attitude made us really angry. We all jumped on him and when we held him we realised he had a mobile phone and money. One of my friends said, 'Let's have that'. He couldn't do anything because we were all beating him. One of us took the gear off him and then we let him go and he ran off. He was quite bruised and battered.

It's a Fact that...

◆ People of an Afro-Caribbean or Asian background are more likely to be victims of crime than white people.

Q How did you feel afterwards?

A Immediately afterwards I felt powerful. There was quite an adrenalin flow with the boy and it had been like winning over him. I didn't feel anything about the victim except that he had brought it on himself. And being in a group meant we cheered each other on, and none of us would have wanted to admit to the others that we didn't think it a good thing to have done.

Q Did you think about the victim at all afterwards?

A I felt bad about him. Once I had calmed down and got over the drink I remembered how it felt when I was mugged which was bad. I think it wasn't a nice thing to do. And I don't see it as the way to get kudos as some

kids do. Street robbery is usually a cowardly crime because kids do it in gangs and intimidate their victim. I do feel remorseful. Although I got picked up and am now inside for being with someone who mugged, I won't do it again now I've grown up.

> " Street robbery is usually a cowardly crime because kids do it in gangs and intimidate their victim. "

41

It's a Fact that...

Punishment for a mugging can be one or a combination of the following: a fine, probation, community service, a curfew order or a prison sentence (which may be suspended or may be given immediately).

Q Did the police get involved?

A The boy we mugged went to the police station which is opposite the chip shop in my area. My mates and I went in to have something to eat.

Our victim was reporting what had happened at the police station and he saw us as he was leaving (we were wearing distinctive clothes). The police came over and arrested us and took us to the police station.

Q What happened then?

A I was put in a cell which was horrible and kept there until the morning because they are not allowed to interview juveniles during the early hours. I was transferred to another police station where they asked me what happened and I told them. I pleaded guilty. I had a solicitor because I asked for one but I didn't really understand what was being said. The victim wasn't pressing charges so I was just cautioned. They finger print you, take a photo and do a DNA test. It really makes you feel you've joined the ranks of the criminal.

"I feel that's unfair because I learned my lesson that first time and decided I wasn't going to mug again."

Q So did you stay out of trouble after this?

A I didn't do any more street robbery. Partly it wasn't worth it for something like a phone and a fiver. I knew it wouldn't buy me a new life, which is what I want. I come from a really poor family and it's really hard never being able to have things or do things you see other kids having and doing. But I was with a group of friends and one of them mugged someone and took his phone and wallet. So when the police came and the victim said I had been there I was picked up and charged and because I already had an offence on my sheet they found me guilty. I feel that's unfair because I learned my lesson that first time and decided I wasn't going to mug again.

Q So what happened after you were found guilty?

A I was given an eighteen-month prison sentence which I'm serving now. I'd like to go straight when I come out, but it's much harder after you've been inside and everyone just sees you as a criminal. The stupid thing is part of the reason kids like me start getting into trouble is because we're out of school and bored and broke. If there were more youth clubs and facilities for us we probably wouldn't be out on the streets and staying

"I'd like to go straight when I come out, but it's much harder after you've been inside and everyone just sees you as a criminal."

It's a Fact that...

Black men (under 30) are less likely to commit an offence than young white men.

out late so much. In fact, after the caution I was sent to a special educational unit and through them I went to college. I got qualifications in maths, English, business studies and IT. I might have made something of myself with those if I hadn't been picked up and sent to prison.

Q How does your mother feel about the way things have gone with you?

A She's not happy about it but she doesn't understand what it is like as a young black man - how much people see you as a bad lot and how that affects the way you behave. She can't see things my way, she just thinks I should just settle down and behave. I'll go back to live with her when I get out but that means I'll be back among

all my friends again. There's always the worry I'll get into trouble again because of mixing with them.

Q People tend to think of black young men as being muggers but do they get mugged as well?

A That's one of the really damaging stereotypes about black boys. Sure they do some of it but I know lots of black kids who've been mugged too - myself included - and by white kids.

Talking Points

◆ What sort of area does Denzel come from? Do you think the area he lived in affects his behaviour? How?

◆ Denzel thought at the time that the boy was 'confrontational and aggressive'. Does this justify the group's response?

◆ Denzel thinks that the way people see him has affected his behaviour. Does the way people see you affect your behaviour? Do you think this is a fair reason for the group's attack?

◆ Denzel talks about stereotypes at the end of the interview. Why is 'all young black men are muggers' a stereotype? What could be done to change this?

◆ It's clear that Denzel feels remorse for what he's done. Do you think it would have helped him and the victim if they had met to discuss what happened?

45

Useful addresses and contacts

UK

Victim Support
Charity offering information and support to all victims of crime, except theft of, or from, cars and child abuse in the family.

Cranmer House, 39 Brixton Road,
London SW9 6DZ
Tel: 020 7735 9166, Helpline: 0845 3030 900
www.victimsupport.org

Victim Support Scotland
15/23 Hardwell Close, Edinburgh EH8 9RX
Tel: 0131 668 4486
www.victimsupportsco.demon.co.uk

Crime Concern
Charity working to prevent crime and create safer communities. The website provides an online resource relating to crime reduction.

Beaver House, 147-150 Victoria Road, Swindon,
Wilts, SN1 3UY
Tel: 01793 863 500
www.crimeconcern.org.uk

Crimestoppers
For people who have information about a crime in the UK but wish to remain anonymous.

Freephone: 0800 555 111
www.crimestoppers-uk.org

Samaritans
Voluntary agency providing 24-hour support for people feeling depressed, isolated, or in despair.

Helpline: 08457 90 90 90
www.samaritans.org.uk

VOICE UK
Help for people with learning disabilities who have experienced crime or abuse.

Voice UK, Wyvern House, Railway Terrace,
Derby DE1 2RU
Tel: 01332 295775
www.voiceuk.org.uk

ChildLine
Voluntary agency providing a telephone counselling service for children and young people in danger and distress.

24-hour free helpline: 0800 1111
www.childline.org.uk

Police Services UK
A website which lists official police services and police-related organisations.

www.police.uk

AUSTRALIA

Victim Support - South Australia
11 Halifax Street, Adelaide 5000
Postal address: PO Box 6610, Halifax Street,
Adelaide 5000
Tel: (08) 8231 5626
www.victimsa.org

A full directory of Australian victim support services can be found at:

www.vaonline.org/australasiavs.html

Glossary

adrenalin
A chemical that is released in the body when someone is angry, excited or scared. It makes the heart beat faster.

assault
A violent physical or verbal attack.

bolshie
A slang term for someone who is being confrontational.

community service
Unpaid work that benefits other people. Young offenders sometimes have to perform community service instead of being fined or imprisoned.

counselling
When people talk about a problem or something that is bothering them with someone trained to help them.

curfew
People subject to a curfew must stay indoors from a certain time at night until a certain time in the morning.

DNA test
The pattern of DNA that is different in every person can be analysed in a sample of blood, saliva or tissue. The police can take samples from scenes of crime and can test them to see if they match a suspect's sample.

excluded
Someone who is excluded from school is not allowed to attend it because of bad behaviour.

identification parade
A group of people, one of whom is suspected of committing a crime. A witness is then asked to see if he or she can identify the suspect. Usually the witness cannot be seen by the people in the parade.

mugging
When someone is robbed for their personal possessions, usually in a public place.

offender
Someone who has broken the law.

paranoid
Someone who suspects or distrusts others without justification.

sentence
A punishment given to someone who has been found guilty of a crime.

shocked
A person's emotional and physical state when something unpleasant has happened to them.

solicitor
A lawyer who gives legal advice and prepares cases for court.

stereotype
An idea of what someone or something is like that is fixed and simplistic.

tagged
Someone who has been convicted of a crime can be given a tag which monitors their whereabouts.

Victim Support
An agency that provides help for people who have been a victim of crime.

witness
Someone who appears in a court of law to say what they know about a crime.

youth court
A court for people who are accused of a crime when they are under 18. Access for the public and press is restricted. The defendant and any witness under 18 cannot be identified. Child witnesses can give videotaped evidence to avoid direct court appearances.

Youth Offending Team (YOT)
A team of people from social services, police, probation, education and health whose aim is to help young offenders and prevent them reoffending. Teams are based throughout England and Wales.

Index

Getting active!

On your own:
Imagine you have been asked to make a television documentary about the experiences of the people in this book. What would you bring in to it as well as interviews with the people involved? Who else would you interview? Who could give you more information? Write a plan for the documentary, including ideas for each scene.

In pairs:
Think about and research how you could reduce crime and improve personal safety in your area. Put together an action plan.

In groups:
Role play one of the case studies, with one person being the victim and the others playing the attackers and other people involved where necessary. Does the role play help you understand the motivations and feelings of the people involved? Practise first and then record your scene.